Curriculum Development and Assessment

Integrating AI

3rd edition

Formerly: A Guidebook for Course Development and Assessment 2nd Edition

Rick Upchurch

Tools to Lead Publishing

CURRICULUM DEVELOPMENT AND ASSESSMENT 3RD EDITION

Copyright © 2025 by Rick Upchurch: rlupchurch@gmail.com

Published by Tools to Lead Publishing

Printed in the United States of America

All rights reserved. No part of this publication may be reproduced, stored in a retrieval system or transmitted in any form or by any means – for example, electronic, photocopy, recording – without prior written permission of the author. The only exception is brief quotations for research purposes.

ISBN: 978-0-9833239-7-6

TABLE OF CONTENTS

Chapter 1 - Introduction 1
    The Problem 3
    The Solution 5
Chapter 2 - The Course Description 7
    Artificial Intelligence Tip 9
Chapter 3 - Course Objective/Competency 11
    Weekly Learning Objectives 16
    Artificial Intelligence Tip 20
Chapter 4 - A Taxonomy for Learning. 21
Chapter 5 – Cognigitve load 27
    Intrinsic Load 28
    Extraneous Load 28
    Germane Load 29
    Balancing the Three Types of Load 30
    Cognitive Load and Christian Worldview Integration 31
    Cognitive Load and Artificial Intelligence 31
        Summary 32
Chapter 6 - Assignments 33
    Balance 33
    Relationship of Assignments to Course Objectives 37
    Relationship of Assignments to Taxonomy of Learning 38
        Summary 41
Chapter 7 - Learning Activities 43
    Sample Learning Activities 46
    Artificial Intelligence Tip 47
Chapter 8 - Assessment 49
Chapter 9 - Faith Integration 51

    Artificial Intelligence Tip 54

Chapter 10 – Calculating Seat Time 55

    Artificial Intelligence Tip 62

Chapter 11 - Step-by-step Instructions for Using the Curriculum Audit 63

    Section A 63

    Section B 64

    Section C 67

    Section D 70

    Section E 70

Chapter 12 - Online Variations 71

    Using the U-CATO to help develop and audit the online course 81

Chapter 13 - Conclusion 85

Conceptual Model for Curriculum Development Including and Using Generative AI for Curriculum Development 89

    The Four-Part Model 89

    How the Model Facilitates Student Preparedness 91

    Addendum: Using Generative AI in Curriculum Development 93

        Prompts for Course Development: 93

        prompts 94

Bibliography 97

CHAPTER 1 - INTRODUCTION

This book is designed for individuals charged with preparing and teaching a course, or for those responsible for developing curriculum. The focus is on the pragmatic application of course development principles. The material in this book will be an invaluable aid for improving the quality and functionality of any curriculum. While the material in this book may be applicable to any teaching experience, it is primarily intended for those teaching college-level courses.

Unfortunately, the fact of the matter is that most of those teaching in higher education have received little to no instruction on how to teach. They are usually experts in their subject matter, yet approach the teaching task armed only with the experiences they have had in the classroom. In some cases, those experiences have provided insight into effective learning, but more often than not, they have left memories of methods and practices to avoid. Most college instructors default to their teaching style, which is often based on what they observed from their professors, without regard for whether this is the most effective method of instruction, and often without awareness that other methods even exist.

Part of the problem faced in this scenario is the lack of a personal educational philosophy that clearly describes the intent of the instructional process. To put this in the simplest terms: is the instruction to be an impartation of knowledge by a properly prepared and credentialed instructor, or is the focus on the acquisition of knowledge by the student? This is the classic "sage on the stage" versus "guide on the side" debate. On the surface, this disparity might seem the same, but in the first case, the instructor's job is to ensure the material is covered sufficiently to qualify as a "college" course. *The most important consideration for this model is covering the assigned material.*

In the second case, the "guide on the side" model emphasizes student learning. It does not necessarily mean covering less material, but it does mean covering the material in a way that students grasp the concepts and can integrate the knowledge more fully into their gestalt. This model requires more than subject matter knowledge; it also requires effort in determining which teaching methods should be used to communicate the information effectively, ensuring that student learning occurs. *Without negating the importance of the instructor and their credentials, the focus of this model is squarely on the student and their learning experience.* This philosophical perspective is a crucial one. Every institution will ideally make decisions about what is part of its philosophy and clearly articulate them to its faculty.

THE PROBLEM

Most syllabi, let alone complete curricula, do not undergo a standardized review process to ensure an acceptable level of quality. That may seem surprising, even shocking, but it is true. For those who teach in the traditional classroom, there is often no evaluation of the syllabi or discussion of curricular issues. For online programs, a curriculum development process is typically in place; however, in most cases, it does not include a qualitative analysis of the curriculum against the institution's educational philosophy and best practices. In best-case scenarios, the curriculum is developed by subject matter experts using a template with agreed-upon pieces already inserted in an approved format.

In some cases, the curriculum is reviewed by an administrator who may not have the time or understanding needed to evaluate its quality. In the worst case, Subject Matter Experts (SMEs) develop a course with little or no guidance on what it should look like or how it fits into the overall academic program. Perhaps there is an old syllabus to follow, but little guidance is given, or available, to the course writer, since everyone is already too busy developing their own course. Even where a template exists, there is considerable variation from institution to institution and sometimes even within an institution regarding the most essential ingredients of a well-written curriculum.

Here are some of the problems I have observed:
- No template provided, or only the barest framework – this allows the SME the most freedom to design the course as they choose.

Unfortunately, the implication is that there are no boundaries when, in fact, there *are* boundaries; they are just unwritten. Without a template of any kind, SME can feel deserted and alone at one end of the continuum, or all-powerful at the other. In this situation, connections between course objectives and material are often inconsistent. For online programs that rely on consistency of format for improved student interaction/retention, this model presents unique challenges to program integrity and achieving outcomes at every level.

- No attempt to evaluate homework for load or an absence of guidelines related to appropriate load – this may sound trivial, but one of the most significant complaints students have is that some weeks the homework is too heavy and other weeks the homework is almost non-existent.
- No guidance on how to write appropriate course objectives – the ability to write effective course objectives is often overlooked, especially by new faculty. These course objectives, if well-written, can direct the course's flow like the riverbanks guide the water to the ocean. Appropriately, written course objectives align with the program's and the institution's overall objectives. The course becomes part of a whole garment tailored to fit the institution's mission and the student's needs.
- No attempt to evaluate homework against course objectives.
- No attempt to evaluate homework against an accepted learning model.
- No attempt to evaluate learning activities against course objectives.
- Little or no attempt to evaluate learning activities against an accepted learning model.

- Little or no attempt to evaluate learning activities against appropriate educational methodology.
- No clear explanation of how the course objectives should be measured for success.
- There is a misunderstanding of faith integration for faith-based institutions, which is either superficial or ignored.

THE SOLUTION

The premise of this book is an educational philosophy based on a student-centered learning model. The material presented herein will examine practical ways instructors can design courses to enhance the likelihood of student learning. Using this information will equip the course writer to be more effective in avoiding the pitfalls, which are part of the higher education landscape, and, more importantly, provide students with a superior educational experience.

The impetus for this work stems from the development of a tool that addresses the aforementioned concerns. That tool is the U-CAT, also known as the Upchurch Curriculum Audit Tool, or the U-CATO for online courses. The U-CAT allows the course developer to evaluate a course against various standards. Using the information from the U-CAT, the course developer can focus on relevant areas and develop a more integrated and balanced curriculum. With this tool, writers can identify problem areas at a glance and then address them. The use of this tool is crucial for anyone who is writing a new course or modifying an existing one. The U-CAT can also be an invaluable aid in evaluating curriculum. It is a tool that has value for the novice and the experienced course writer. Administrators can use the U-CAT to review curriculum relative to the institution's educational philosophy and other expectations.

The Curriculum Audit is described in detail later and is available for free online at https://tinyurl.com/28sl2klj . Please feel free to modify the UCAT or the UCATO to meet the needs of your institution.

The topics below and their relevance for curriculum development and assessment will be examined. The differences between curricula delivered in the classroom and online will be discussed, with the differences noted.

- The Course Description – start with the end in mind
- Course Objective (learning outcomes)
- A Taxonomy for Learning
- Assignments
- Learning Activities
- Instructional style
- Assessment
- Faith Integration
- Calculating Seat Time
- Curriculum Audit

CHAPTER 2 - THE COURSE DESCRIPTION

The Course Description (CD) is what the student sees in the catalog and often is the deciding factor in whether or not to take the course. The inclusion of the CD in the catalog provides a type of "agreement" between the student and the institution that should not be taken lightly. Often, students remark in the post-class evaluation, complaining about the lack of direct connection between the CD and what was actually covered in the course. It is wise, therefore, to focus upon clearly understanding the course description BEFORE starting work on the course design. It is essential to examine the CD carefully and, if necessary, dissect it to fully understand the implications of the description. The CD provides the boundaries for the course, and those boundaries must be observed to avoid problems and possible challenges. If, for any reason, the CD is no longer aligned with the division/institution's needs, there is likely an approved process in place for modification. However, such modifications can often take weeks, if not months, to take effect, meaning that, regardless of the instructor/writer's inclinations, the course may have to be taught based on the existing CD in the short run.

In the case where the CD has not been written, it is wise to write the CD in such a way that it is descriptive without placing too many constrictions upon the course. This can allow for easier modification as the course evolves without the hassle of going through a change process. Here is an example of a CD, which demonstrates the point above:

Well Written:	Poorly Written:
Philosophy of Religion - Study and discussion of a broad range of issues in the philosophy of religion, such as religious epistemology, the ontological argument, the cosmological argument, the teleological argument, religion and science, and the problem of evil.	**Philosophy of Religion** – A consideration of various attempts to provide a philosophical formulation and defense of the basic tenets of the theistic worldview, with particular attention to recent analytic philosophy.

In the well-written example, the inclusion of "such as" leaves room for the course to be easily modified while simultaneously giving a sense of what the course will cover. In the poorly written example, the words "theistic" and "recent analytical philosophy" reflect a too narrow focus, which is out of line with the title of the course, in that the scope of "Philosophy of Religion" is a much broader topic than the proposed focus.

Here are three things to keep in mind when writing a CD:
1. The course title should be reflected in the course description. This may seem obvious, but too often, the course description appears to have no connection to the title, confusing students and compromising the integrity of the catalog, and possibly the institution.

2. The course description should contain enough particulars to allow the reader to get a feel for what the course will cover, without being too specific. There needs to be room in the CD for some latitude on the part of the instructor teaching the course, and still fulfill the CD.
3. The course description should be written in a style that, ideally, would entice the reader to enroll in the course, keeping in mind the two points above. Styles evolve, but a good rule of thumb is to match the complexity of the course description to the course level. For instance, a freshman course would have less technical jargon and be written in a more accessible style than a senior-level course.

ARTIFICIAL INTELLIGENCE TIP

Artificial intelligence can provide a good course description when using a well-written prompt, such as:

> *If the course doesn't have a description,* **Prompt**: Act as if you have a Ph.D in XXX and are developing an online college course titled XXX, at the XXX (Freshman, Sophomore, Junior, Senior, Graduate, Doctoral) level, create a 3-6 sentence description. The description should be professional but interesting enough to encourage student enrollment.

This prompt, as well as others, can be found in the Addendum at the end of this book.

> NOTE: Once you have the course description, you can use that along with my automated GPT/GEM instructions to create the syllabus, including course competencies, assignments, readings, etc. You can purchase the instructions for building the GPT here: https://app.lemonsqueezy.com/share/707101 .

CHAPTER 3 - COURSE OBJECTIVE/COMPETENCY

The inclusion of Course Objectives/Competencies is often viewed by some as one of those things required by administrators, which has little or no value to the course itself. This is an unfortunate perspective, as well-written course objectives can effectively guide the development of the curriculum, making it more focused and effective. *The secret here is that for this to happen, the course objectives have to be well-written.* The writing of course objectives requires the ability to step back from the trees to gain a clear view of the forest. When viewed from this perspective, the objectives should have a holistic feel, identifying the learning that should occur as a result of completing the course, which aligns with the course description.

How does one write an effective course objective? The secret is in two parts. The first part concerns understanding the concept of the "irreducible minimum." The "irreducible minimum" is a concept proposed by Bruce Wilkinson in his book *The Seven Laws of the Learner.* He says that in any course, some of the content is more important than other parts, i.e. there is some learning that is crucial to the successful completion of the course. Wilkinson would say this applies not only to the *design* of the course objectives but also equally to the actual class *sessions.*

The ability to categorize the expected learning into six to eight statements provides a focus, which effectively steers the curriculum through the maze of information deluge. Unfortunately, this sounds easier than it may actually be. I have seen lists of up to 20 different course objectives proposed by course writers who genuinely believed that each one was crucial to the course. There are two things that happen in cases like this: either the learning is so shallow and/or fragmented that little is actually retained, or the 20 objectives are, in reality, subpoints under four to six comprehensive objectives. If the first is true, then the course writer needs to be counseled as to the reality of what is actually doable within the course boundaries. In this case, the homework load area of the U-CAT can be an invaluable guide to demonstrate that too much is being required. If the second is true, then it is just a matter of grouping the terms and writing course objectives, which are less specific but accomplish the same goals.

The second part concerns the choice of words used to compose the course objective. It might seem as if this is also an exercise easily accomplished, but that is misleading. I would have to say that composing clear, measurable course objectives is an area where most course writers struggle. Several considerations influence the choice of words used to formulate an effective course objective.

Here are some basic principles

- Have an action word that describes what the student will *do* differently because of your course.
- Describe meaningful learning.

- Be measured/verified; i.e., you can measure students' ability to achieve them.
- Represent high levels of thinking, rather than trivial tasks.
- Be written in plain language that students can understand.

Probably the best way to do this is to have a list of appropriate action words beside you as you are writing the objectives. I highly recommend using terms from the taxonomy listed in the next section when composing the course objectives. Words such as the following have been found to be good choices when developing course objectives:

Construct	Critique
Summarize	Communicate
Explain	Classify
Analyze	Compare
Differentiate	Articulate
Organize	Evaluate
Define	Understand

One word of caution here: Some institutions frown on the use of the word "understand" in course objectives since it is notoriously difficult to evaluate exactly what anyone truly "understands."

Objectives for the course are typically introduced with a statement such as "Upon completion of this course, the student should be able to:" The use of the word "should" is debated by some who believe a better choice is "will." The difference is significant. When using "should," the objective can be evaluated, but there is no guarantee that learning will occur in each case. Using the word "will" places a significantly greater burden on the teaching/learning process, as it asserts that the student will be able to be positively evaluated for their successful achievement of the stated objective. I urge institutions to use "should" unless a strong curricular and assessment process is in place, which can address discrepancies.

Whether "should," "will," or some other term is employed, the course objectives listed under this statement describe the focus of the learning, which is planned for that course. For example, a course on Adult Development and Life Assessment could have the following objectives:

> Upon successful completion of this course, adult learners should be able to:
>
> 1. Articulate personal worldview assumptions and relate those assumptions to life and career development
> 2. Demonstrate knowledge and application of classical and contemporary adult development theory
> 3. Demonstrate awareness of personal strengths and relate those strengths to life and career development
> 4. Demonstrate confidence in anticipating and managing adult transitions through lifelong learning

Let us see how these fulfill the requirements for effective course objectives:

> First, does each of the objectives have an action word that describes what the student will DO differently because of completing the course? The action words used are "articulate" and "demonstrate." Although there is possibly too much dependence upon the word "demonstrate,"

the objectives clearly indicate what the student should be able to "do differently" because of the course.

Second, do the objectives describe meaningful learning? For objective #1, students will need to become aware of their personal worldview and how it relates to their life goals – this appears to be meaningful learning. For objective #2, students will become aware of adult learning theory and demonstrate this awareness. Since this class is designed for adults, the acquisition of that knowledge should conceivably assist the student in future learning endeavors: again, this seems like meaningful learning. For objective #3, the students will demonstrate an awareness of their personal strengths, especially as they relate to their career and personal development. Whenever a student becomes more self-aware and can demonstrate how that awareness affects their life, it should be considered meaningful learning. For objective #4, the expectation is that students will demonstrate confidence and anticipation in managing adult transitions through lifelong learning. This objective may not describe meaningful learning that is unique to the other objectives and could be combined with Objective #2. Additionally, this fourth objective will be challenging to measure, as it is unclear whether it has been achieved, which is the next point.

Third, the objectives should be measurable and verifiable; i.e., you can measure students' ability to achieve them. This kind of assessment can be designed for the first three objectives in the example, but not for the fourth objective.

Fourth and finally, the objectives should represent high levels of thinking, rather than trivial tasks. All four objectives qualify under this guideline.

Outcome statements that meet all of the above criteria are sometimes challenging to craft alone. A good practice is to collaborate with a peer or Department Chair/Dean when crafting course objectives. With practice, you should be able to get your ideas down to a few clearly written statements that define the purpose of the course for you and your students.

There is a place on the U-CAT for the course objectives to be listed along with an associated code letter, which will be explained in detail later.

WEEKLY LEARNING OBJECTIVES

Although not specifically connected to the U-CAT, a well-written course will not only have course objectives that span the entire learning experience, but will also have weekly learning objectives, which can be thought of as tactical units that support and contribute to achieving the course objectives. There are usually about 2–4 weekly objectives, depending on the length of the class session. These objectives provide the boundaries into which the river of learning should flow for the duration of a specific class session. When developing the course, the first step after completing the course objectives is to map those objectives over the course duration, using a sequencing model.

Think of a sequencing model as the strategic plan to accomplish the course objectives. As with any strategic plan, there are individual, tactical goals that lead in an organized fashion to the accomplishment of the overall plan (course objectives). The sequencing model can be derived from personal experience, a textbook, or other sources. Its purpose is to guide the student through the material in a manner that fosters learning and fulfills the course objectives. The mapping of course objectives onto this model enables the course writer to ensure that nothing is missed. In some cases, a course objective will be connected to one week, while another course objective may show up connected to every week. *The important thing is that each objective connects somewhere.* Using the example above of the Adult Development and Life Assessment course and a sequencing model based on following the structure of the textbooks used in the course, a reasonable map would look like the diagram below. Note that while only two sessions, or class meetings, are mentioned in the example, the principle needs to be repeated, with each session objective mapped back to a course objective:

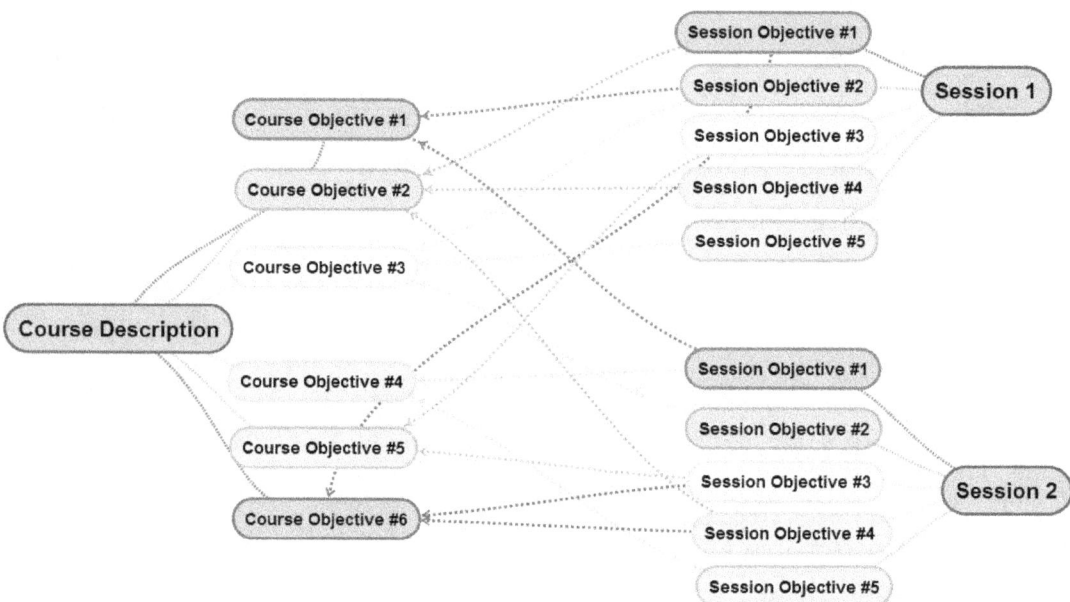

The weekly learning objectives should be relatively few in number and written in a similar fashion to the course objectives, except that they focus on achieving the learning targeted for that specific class session.

For example, the course objectives for a course in Biblical Covenants might be:

> Upon completion of this course, the students should be able to:
> 1. Define covenant, the various types of biblical covenants and their significance.
> 2. Describe the major points of the key biblical covenants: Abrahamic, Mosaic, Davidic, and New.
> 3. Communicate God's redemptive nature and acts using biblical examples from various covenants.
> 4. Use the covenant paradigm as a hermeneutic for understanding and interpreting scripture.

5. Evaluate his/her own personal participation in a covenant relationship with God.

A set of *weekly*[1] learning objectives connected to this same course could be:

Weekly Objectives – Week #1:
1. The student will be able to define covenant within a biblical context. (Mapped to #1 and #2 above)
2. The student will be able to describe the particulars of a covenant relationship in broad categories. (Mapped to #2 above)
3. The student will be able to explain how the covenants provide a unifying theme for understanding how God has and is working with humankind. (Mapped to #3 above)

As you can see, the course objectives #1, 2, and 3 are touched upon in this week's objectives. Once the objectives are defined, it is simply a matter of determining what should be assigned to accomplish those objectives and which in-class learning activities will best reinforce that learning.

By following these steps, it is possible to design specific class session objectives that align with and support the broader course objectives. At first, this kind of work may seem too complicated or even confusing, but after working with this process for several years and involving hundreds of faculty members, I am convinced that it is one of the greatest needs of our educational system.

---

[1] Note this is only one week's learning objectives.

Fortunately, this type of mapping can be easily accomplished through the use of artificial intelligence. I have included a prompt for this purpose in the Addendum at the end of this book.

ARTIFICIAL INTELLIGENCE TIP

Artificial intelligence can provide a good course description when using a well-written prompt, such as:

> *Course Competencies,* **Prompt**: Act as if you have a Ph.D in XXX and are developing an online college course titled XXX, at the XXX (Freshman, Sophomore, Junior, Senior, Graduate, Doctoral) level, suggest 8-10 Student competencies that complete this sentence: At the conclusion of this course, the student should be able to. Do not use the word understand. One of the course competencies should focus on integrating the course into a Christian worldview. One of the competencies should be the ability to effectively utilize generative AI in the subject area.
> a. *Note that you must carefully edit these competencies to match your vision for the course.*

This prompt, as well as others, can be found in the Addendum at the end of this book.

CHAPTER 4 - A TAXONOMY FOR LEARNING.

The original Bloom's taxonomy provided a way to evaluate both the learning plan and the learning accomplished. Bloom's hierarchy of learning levels has effectively guided course development for decades and has had a profound impact on the educational system. The descriptive terms of the taxonomy have made it possible to view learning using a graduated scale of lower-level vs higher-level thinking/learning. With the use of this tool, it has been possible to guide students into higher levels of learning through appropriate learning activities and assignments.

Anderson has revisited Bloom's taxonomy and made some modifications, which raise the effectiveness of the tool to a new level. In Bloom's original taxonomy, the major emphasis was on the cognitive functions. Within this domain, the descriptive terms identified the various levels of thinking. In Anderson's revision (Anderson, p.5), the taxonomy has been expanded into a two-dimensional matrix, which connects the various levels in two dimensions: the cognitive process dimension and the knowledge dimension.

In the cognitive dimension, there are six categories: remember, understand, apply, analyze, evaluate, and create. Think of the categories of the cognitive process dimension as column headings on a spreadsheet. In the knowledge dimension, there are four categories: factual, conceptual, procedural, and meta-cognitive. Think of the categories of the knowledge dimension as the rows of the spreadsheet.

	The Cognitive Process Dimension					
The Knowledge Dimension	1. Remember	2. Understand	3. Apply	4. Analyze	5. Evaluate	6. Create
A. Factual Knowledge	X					
B. Conceptual Knowledge						
C. Procedural Knowledge						
D. Meta-Cognitive Knowledge						

Each learning experience would then be categorized on the knowledge dimension as factual, conceptual, procedural, or meta-cognitive (a combination of the others) and correlated with one of the categories from the cognitive process dimension. For example, a learning experience can be both factual (knowledge dimension) and a cognitive process (cognitive process dimension). An example would be learning vocabulary.

Although the U-CAT focuses on the cognitive process dimension and the categories associated with it, regardless of the knowledge dimension, it is worth remembering that the categories of the knowledge dimension still influence learning.

Here are the levels, which Anderson has identified from the lowest to the highest level in the cognitive process dimension:

Remembering: Retrieving, recognizing, and recalling relevant knowledge from long-term memory.
Understanding: Constructing meaning from oral, written, and graphic messages through interpreting, exemplifying, classifying, summarizing, inferring, comparing, and explaining.
Applying: Carrying out or using a procedure through executing, or implementing.
Analyzing: Breaking material into constituent parts, determining how the parts relate to one another and to an overall structure or purpose through differentiating, organizing, and attributing.
Evaluating: Making judgments based on criteria and standards through checking and critiquing.
Creating: Putting elements together to form a coherent or functional whole; reorganizing elements into a new pattern or structure through generating, planning, or producing.

A well-designed course will take into account the academic status of the student (e.g. first year, sophomore, junior, senior, or graduate student), along with the complexity of the subject to be studied, and gradually lead the student to higher levels of learning. Keep in mind that some courses will be limited to the lower levels of learning by the nature of their subject, just as some will start at and move to ever-higher levels of learning for the same reason. I would argue that in every course, there should be some movement toward higher levels of learning, regardless of the starting point.

The relevance of this discussion arises when the cognitive dimension of the learning taxonomy is linked to the curriculum in two ways.

First, how it affects the learning activities that occur in the classroom. While learning activities are the subject of another chapter, briefly, they can be described as those activities occurring within the boundary of the classroom experience, which the instructor has designed to achieve student learning. By associating each of these activities with some level of the taxonomy of learning, it has the effect of guiding the teaching/learning process to ensure higher levels of learning.

The second application pertains to the homework assigned for the course. The connection of the taxonomy of learning to assigned homework is often neglected, with the assumption that what is assigned actually achieves the goals necessary for learning to occur. What is typical, however, is that the assigned work simply follows the order presented in the book and falls mostly in the lower levels of the taxonomy. The result is that the homework assigned may actually do little to enhance the learning desired.

Therefore, understanding the taxonomy and applying it when considering both learning activities and homework assignments can have a profound impact on the quality of the final curriculum. As will be described later, the U-CAT provides space to associate both learning activities and homework assignments with different categories of the cognitive dimension, making it apparent at a glance their position on the taxonomy.

It also assists the course writer in determining whether the assignments and activities are actually achieving the envisioned goals for students completing the course. In this capacity, the UCAT assists the course writer by identifying those activities or assignments that need to be modified to strengthen the material to meet the desired effect.

CHAPTER 5 – COGNIGITVE LOAD

Cognitive Load Theory (CLT) provides a helpful set of principles for designing curriculum that aligns with how the human mind actually learns. While the taxonomy of learning helps us categorize the *level* of thinking associated with instructional tasks, CLT helps us consider the *mental effort* required from students to successfully engage those tasks. Without thoughtful attention to cognitive load, even well-designed objectives, assignments, and learning activities can unintentionally hinder learning rather than promote it. At its core, CLT distinguishes between three types of cognitive load that operate simultaneously during learning: **intrinsic load**, **extraneous load**, and **germane load**. Each plays a significant role in shaping the student's capacity to process, store, and apply new knowledge. As course writers, our responsibility is not to eliminate cognitive load—learning always requires effort—but to calibrate it so that the learner's effort is focused on meaningful learning rather than unnecessary confusion or fatigue.

Because cognitive load directly influences both instructional design and the student experience, its principles naturally align with the student-centered philosophy described in the opening chapter. Instructors who understand and manage cognitive load intentionally create conditions where deeper learning becomes not only possible but more probable.

INTRINSIC LOAD

Intrinsic load refers to the inherent complexity of the material itself. Some subjects are inherently more complex than others, and certain tasks necessitate the simultaneous integration of multiple concepts. For example, solving a multistep calculus problem or conducting a theological analysis of a biblical covenant requires coordinating several interrelated pieces of information. Intrinsic load cannot be removed, but it *can be managed*. This management occurs when the instructor sequences material thoughtfully, scaffolds learning in appropriate increments, and avoids assuming prior knowledge that students may not yet possess. Understanding the "irreducible minimum" discussed earlier becomes especially useful here. When course writers identify what is truly essential, they can focus cognitive effort on that core learning rather than overwhelm students with secondary details.

Questions for course writers:
What are the true conceptual bottlenecks in this course? At what points will students naturally struggle? How might these areas be sequenced differently to foster clarity instead of confusion?

EXTRANEOUS LOAD

Extraneous load arises not from the difficulty of the material, but from the way it is presented. Poorly written instructions, unnecessary complexity, disorganized learning materials, or unclear expectations can dramatically increase cognitive burden. This type of load contributes nothing to learning and should be minimized wherever possible.

Examples of extraneous load include lengthy assignment prompts that obscure rather than clarify expectations, lecture slides crowded with text, or weekly structures that force students to search across multiple documents to understand what to do. The U-CAT is specifically designed to expose these issues by aligning learning activities, assignments, and outcomes with precision. When instructors make those connections explicit, extraneous load diminishes and student success increases.

Reducing extraneous load is not an act of "lowering rigor." It is a commitment to clarity for the sake of deep learning.

GERMANE LOAD

Germane load represents the mental effort students devote to processing, organizing, and integrating new knowledge — the very heart of learning. While intrinsic and extraneous load must be managed, germane load should be encouraged. Learning activities that foster reflection, application, comparison, analysis, and synthesis directly support germane load and align naturally with the higher levels of the taxonomy.

Assignments that require students to articulate their thinking, solve novel problems, or integrate Christian worldview considerations often increase germane load in productive ways. Germane load is evidence that students are not merely remembering content but transforming it into part of their internal schema.

The task for the course writer is to ensure that germane load is *not competing* with excessive intrinsic or extraneous load. When all three types of load are in balance, students flourish.

BALANCING THE THREE TYPES OF LOAD

In designing curriculum, the interplay of these three loads must be considered holistically. Too much intrinsic load too early overwhelms students. Too much extraneous load frustrates them. Too little germane load results in shallow learning.

Several practical strategies can promote balance:
- Break complex tasks into sequenced steps.
- Use consistent organizational structures each week.
- Provide models or exemplars of expected work.
- Remove any instructions or resources that do not directly support learning outcomes.
- Design activities that invite students into meaningful cognitive engagement rather than passive consumption.
- Map cognitive load awareness onto the U-CAT so that high-intensity weeks can be identified and adjusted.

A student-centered philosophy disciplines us to evaluate not simply the content to be covered, but the mental effort required to engage that content well.

COGNITIVE LOAD AND CHRISTIAN WORLDVIEW INTEGRATION

For faith-based institutions, managing cognitive load also supports our larger mission. When students feel overwhelmed or confused, they have little cognitive space for reflection on meaning, purpose, or worldview. When load is well balanced, students are more able to engage questions of significance, justice, stewardship, and calling.

Good pedagogy becomes an act of hospitality—an invitation into learning that honors the dignity and limitations of human cognition.

COGNITIVE LOAD AND ARTIFICIAL INTELLIGENCE

Generative AI introduces new possibilities for managing cognitive load. AI can help reduce extraneous load by summarizing texts, clarifying instructions, rewriting confusing prompts, or generating scaffolds for complex assignments. However, AI can also unintentionally increase extraneous load if used without careful design—for example, by producing overly complex materials or offering inconsistent wording across assignments.

Course writers should consider AI a tool for refinement and clarity, not a substitute for thoughtful instructional design. As with all teaching aids, its value depends on the wisdom of its use.

SUMMARY

The intentional management of cognitive load strengthens every component of curriculum design. When cognitive load aligns with course objectives, when assignments and learning activities are calibrated to the learner's capacity, and when extraneous barriers are removed, learning becomes both more effective and more humane.

Curriculum designed with cognitive load in mind becomes a gift to students—a structure that supports them, challenges them appropriately, and frees them to engage deeply with the subject matter and its implications for life, vocation, and faith.

CHAPTER 6 - ASSIGNMENTS

Every course will have assignments that have to be completed outside of class. The concern of this chapter can be divided into three areas:

- balance,
- relationship of assignments to course objectives, and
- relationship of assignments to the taxonomy of learning.

BALANCE

The balance of the amount of homework from week to week, as gauged by the time required to complete the assignments. Balance is typically overlooked by the course developer or given only cursory thought, but has a big impact on meeting the course objectives. A lack of reasonable balance is one of the most common complaints of students, i.e. "One week there are 20 hours of homework assigned and the next there are 5, why is that?" The most common reason this occurs is that the individual writing the course has not given sufficient thought to how the homework is balanced from week to week. Contributing to this problem is that there is rarely an established standard to use as a guideline. The U-CAT suggests a "load" based on the entry level of the student (e.g., first year, sophomore, junior, and senior), requiring more homework from those at higher levels to achieve higher levels of learning. The homework levels suggested in the U-CAT are:

a. 100 level courses   = 7-9 hours/week
b. 200 level courses   = 8-10 hours/week
c. 300 level courses   = 9-11 hours/week
d. 400 level courses   = 10-12 hours/week
e. Masters level courses = 15-18 hours/week
f. Doctoral level course = 18+ hours/week

The rationale for this scale is to ease students into the college experience while still maintaining a standard of acceptable academic rigor. However, the important thing here is not the specifics of this scale, but establishing a clearly defined scale that can be used to guide course development. By that, I mean that your institution may adopt a completely different definition of work required for each level; the more important issue is that there is a level of expectation.

In addition to maintaining an appropriate weekly balance, course writers should also consider the cognitive load created by assignments, ensuring that the amount of intrinsic complexity in any given week does not exceed students' capacity to engage meaningfully with the material. There must also exist other definitions regarding the amount of time it takes for assignments related to reading, writing, research, project completion, etc. The U-CAT suggests standards in two areas, but each institution should consider further definitions; more on this in Chapter 9 on Calculating Seat-Time. The standards set by default in the UCAT are:

a. That assigned reading be calculated at 10 pages per hour and slightly less if the material is highly technical.
b. That written work be calculated at two pages per hour.

The standards suggested above have been determined through experience working with students over several years. These may or may not coincide with your institution's experience or research. Here again, whether or not your institution adopts the same scale is not important. *What is important is that there is an accepted scale.* This allows the course writer to evaluate assignments in relation to the program's expectations.

Using this scale, when 100 pages are assigned to be read, the time calculated for the average student to complete the reading would be approximately 10 hours; if you assigned 300 pages, it could reasonably be expected to take 30 hours for the average student to complete that reading. Remembering the scale provided earlier in this chapter of the number of hours to be assigned outside of class, it is immediately apparent that there is a conflict between the standard and the assignment. What happens when this much reading is assigned is that students make value judgments based on what they feel is "fair" and the other commitments in their lives. If they believe they don't have much time to devote to their homework, instead of reading the assigned pages, they will, at best, skim the material or, at worst, not read it at all.

Honestly, we probably did the same when we were in their shoes. Realistically, if you want students to complete the assignments, they must fit within reasonable boundaries. As a course writer and/or instructor, you may not like this and say, "That's just too bad; the students will have to complete what has been assigned." Some students will complain and complete the work . . . most will not. This goes back to the basic educational philosophy: Subject Dissemination or Student Learning. An extensive extraneous load – whether through unclear instructions, fragmented materials, or overly dense reading – can unintentionally shift the student experience from meaningful engagement to cognitive fatigue, directly undermining learning outcomes.

If you need to assign 300 pages, you are better off assigning those pages to be "skimmed" for discussion in class, breaking them up and assigning different sections to groups to bring back a summary, or some other strategy, which keeps the assignment within a "reasonable" boundary. No one benefits from "over-assignment," and yet this is one of the most common errors of course writing.

I cannot overemphasize the importance of the concept of "fair" within the mind of the average American student. Violation of that concept may be accepted occasionally, but an institution that consistently violates it by assigning homework that cannot be accomplished within the nebulous "fair" parameter will suffer lower retention rates or a lower quality of student work, often accompanied by grade inflation to compensate, or both.

The U-CAT has space for the writer to list the assignments, in abbreviated form, along with the approximate amount of time required to complete those assignments. The times should be added in hour measurements, for instance, 1 hour, 1.3 hours, 1.6 hours, etc. The U-CAT automatically calculates the times for the week and averages them over the entire course, allowing the course writer to easily gauge whether there is an appropriate balance from week to week. An average of 9 hours a week for the course as a whole may seem reasonable until you notice that the maximum for one week is 16 hours and the minimum in another week is only 4 hours. Ideally, the variation between the maximum and minimum should not exceed four hours and preferably not more than two hours. The goal is to balance the work assigned across all the weeks to fit the overall expectation for the course.

RELATIONSHIP OF ASSIGNMENTS TO COURSE OBJECTIVES

Because each assignment contributes to students' overall cognitive load, aligning assignments with course objectives not only ensures relevance but also prevents the addition of unnecessary tasks that increase extraneous load without deepening learning. *Homework must relate to the learning outcomes, or it is a meaningless exercise.* That may seem obvious, but I have reviewed enough curriculum to know that in some cases, what has been assigned has nothing to do with the established learning outcomes. It might be a great learning exercise or a truly profound lecture; it might be a favorite assignment or topic for the Instructor. Regardless, if it does not clearly connect to the learning outcomes for that course, it should not be included.

The U-CAT allows space, on the same line as that used to calculate the time required to complete the course, to indicate which learning outcome(s) apply. By requiring each assignment to be linked to one or more learning outcomes, the curriculum becomes more focused in its ability to facilitate the learning for which it was intended and better able to guide the course writer in the choice of assignments.

RELATIONSHIP OF ASSIGNMENTS TO TAXONOMY OF LEARNING

The taxonomy of learning interacts naturally with cognitive load principles, since higher-order tasks increase germane load in productive ways when designed well, but can overwhelm students when paired with excessive intrinsic or extraneous load. The taxonomy of learning and its value in gauging the impact of assignments on learning were discussed in the previous chapter. There is another space on the U-CAT for making this association. By making the association between the assignment and the taxonomy, it becomes possible to determine the value of the homework as it relates to levels of critical thinking. It has been my experience that much of the homework assigned beyond the reading or watching a lecture, both of which are at the lower level of the taxonomy, is typically written work. Written work that demands a high time commitment, but at lower levels of critical thinking, often results in simply regurgitating the reading. In some cases, it may even be defined as "busy work," which students deplore. The challenge that faces the course writer is how to be creative in designing assignments that achieve the learning outcomes, while also fostering critical thinking, all within a reasonable timeframe. I have included some suggestions below, which may help the course writer think creatively about the types of assignments to be created.

Suggestions:

- For reading assignments:

- The instructor writes a summary paper covering a larger reading assignment and assigns students to read this instead. Students can then be asked to:
    - Summarize the material in their own words.
    - Apply the information to a separate case
    - Create a quiz based on the reading
    - Suggest possible outcomes if some of the information was changed, e.g., in the battle of Gettysburg, would a change in the weather have affected the outcome? How? Why?
  - Assign smaller portions to different students or groups of students with the requirement to condense the reading into abstracts, which are posted to the course Learning Management System (LMS). If this method were used, randomly selecting some questions from this material for a quiz would be recommended.
  - Determine which part of the reading falls within the "irreducible minimum" and assign only those pages, using some of the suggestions below to augment the learning.
- While it is impossible to completely eliminate reading, nor should you, here are some alternative assignments to use to replace some of the reading assignments, if necessary, to keep the homework within the prescribed time limits. Determine the "irreducible minimum" from the reading and alternate ways to achieve that learning. For instance:
  - watching a movie and writing a summary – or applying learning to the viewed material,
  - creating a playlist on youtube.com for students to watch,

- have students create a playlist of a designated number of clips on youtube.com, which support the topic and explain how each one contributes to the topic.
- have students create a YouTube.com video themselves, demonstrating and/or explaining the concepts under discussion. Variation: Once the student's video is posted, have other students analyze it against a rubric. Some students could post the video in the first week, while others analyze, and then swap next week.
- assign an interview – e.g., when discussing history/sociology, interview someone in their 70s about their life as a child and how the world has changed.
- create a class blog and have students post related stories from the internet about the subject under discussion, and make comments analyzing the article against a rubric provided by the instructor.
- create a class wiki and have students develop extensive hyperlinked documents around a central topic.
- assign the students to apply a principle to some aspect of their life and record the results in either a paper, vlogs, or blog. Variation: have them analyze the results, modify their approach, and re-try, with a follow-up report.

When reviewed through both the taxonomy and cognitive load lens, assignments become more than tasks to complete—they become carefully calibrated opportunities for students to construct, refine, and integrate knowledge without exceeding their cognitive capacity.

SUMMARY

Most courses are defined by the in-class activities and the out-of-class assignments. Paying attention to the three considerations in this chapter will positively affect the quality of the curriculum for the course and facilitate student learning at higher levels of critical thinking.

CHAPTER 7 - LEARNING ACTIVITIES

Learning activities are those designed specifically to achieve student learning within the learning environment, either onsite, online (asynchronous), synchronous (but not geographically together), or a combination of all three. Examples of these learning activities include lectures, videos, panel discussions, collaborative software, chats, and video conferencing. Learning activities are *the* heart of the teaching process. Because learning activities shape the real-time cognitive experience of students, each activity should be designed with attention to intrinsic, extraneous, and germane load to ensure that cognitive effort is directed toward meaningful learning rather than unnecessary confusion. Here is where the fruit of the curriculum design has the potential to grow. The implementation of learning activities in instructional design is an expanding field of opportunity, limited only by the instructor's and instructional designer's imagination.

Similar to the chapter above, this area can be divided into three areas of concern: two that correlate and one that is new.

The first concern is how the learning activities are connected to the course objectives. This connection also serves as a checkpoint for managing cognitive load, ensuring that every learning activity requires cognitive effort appropriate to the desired outcome rather than adding avoidable extraneous load. Just as homework must relate to the course objectives or it is a meaningless exercise, so too should the learning activities employed in the classroom/online environment connect to the learning outcomes. The U-CAT provides space to list the learning activity and to associate each activity with at least one learning outcome.

In an earlier section, I discussed learning outcomes, referencing the weekly learning objectives. Although the weekly learning objectives are not listed on the U-CAT, they should be a determining factor in selecting the learning activities. The activities designed to promote learning should be *directly* associated with the weekly learning objectives and easily fit within one or more of the overall course objectives. When this kind of synchronicity occurs, the likelihood of achieving the desired course goal is significantly increased. Faculty who adopt this model will find that their ability to stay on track and focused will be greatly enhanced, which also contributes to student learning. Furthermore, when this model is implemented in a writing curriculum, those using the curriculum will find their task of staying on track easier and produce better results overall.

The second concern relates to associating the learning activities with the taxonomy of learning. There is a space on the U-CAT for making this association. By doing this, it becomes possible to determine the value of the learning activity in relation to the development of critical thinking. Although discussed more fully in the third concern below, the instructional style can significantly affect the level of critical thinking, which is an integral part of a learning activity. For example, although providing a wealth of information, the lecture would typically be considered to offer a lower level of critical thinking skills than a classroom debate or class presentation. By establishing the connection between the activity and the taxonomy of learning, the course writer can determine whether there is sufficient engagement at appropriate levels to facilitate the desired type of learning. When selecting learning activities, instructors should anticipate the cognitive load each activity imposes and, where necessary, provide scaffolding or sequencing to ensure that germane load remains central.

The third concern relates to associating the learning activities with the instructional style that will be used during the allocated time for that activity. Again, there is a space on the U-CAT for making this association. Listed at the end of the U-CAT is a list of possible instructional styles that can be edited by the school to include others as desired. Those listed are:

- L = Lecture, which may or may not include visuals such as PowerPoint, pictures, graphics, objects, etc.
- M = Media, such as video, video clips, audio files, etc.
- C = Collaborative activities, which may include interactive lectures in addition to other options. More on this is included later in this chapter.
- P = Presentations made by students, which can be in the form of a speech, augmented speech with PowerPoint or other visuals, or a student demonstration.

- D = Demonstration made by the instructor or student, usually using some kind of physical process such as an athletic exercise, chemical experiment, step-by-step deconstruction of a passage of literature, working out a math problem on the whiteboard, etc.

An important benefit here is the ability to identify a specific instructional style. For instance, if an institution has set a standard that each course will provide students with the opportunity to make an in-class presentation at least once during each course, it will be easy to scan the list of learning activities and the associated instructional styles to determine if that standard has been met. To do this, simply scan the list of learning activities listed on the U-CAT to see if one has the designation "P" in the "instructional style" column.

SAMPLE LEARNING ACTIVITIES

There is no way any list of learning activities can be truly comprehensive. The following options are included below, some of which seamlessly transition between on-site classroom and online settings.

Sample learning activities:
- Discuss case studies
- Computer simulations w/teams
- Study groups/research projects
- Expert groups
- Issue debates
- Jeopardy w/ class material
- Games/Riddles
- Group create a wiki
- Group creates PowerPoint & presents
- Online threaded comment forums

- peer reviews of papers
- jigsaw (everyone does research & then comes together to fit all parts together)
- role play
- pair share-discussion of the application of visuals in pairs
- tie in life experiences & sharing how it applies to material
- Visual demonstration of theory
- Present themes w/ diff. media (sharing poetry, quotes)
- Brainstorming steps of a process...then order the steps as a group
- Determine the story behind a set of numbers: accounting
- Set a controversial topic...have students choose a point on the schema, then discuss
- Brainstorming
- Groups remember chapter contents from memory
- Collaborate on finding biblical principles in passage
- Brain + mapping/web
- Group engagement on story problems
- How do you do this task in different industries (shared experience)
- Write case studies
- "Zigzag"- rotate tables/each table has a specific question to deal with
- Mock interviews/mock counseling
- Field trips

In our ever-changing environment, new collaborative activities and strategies are constantly being imagined and tested in the classroom. Instructional Designers and Instructors should always be on the lookout for new ways to communicate with the current generation of students.

ARTIFICIAL INTELLIGENCE TIP

Artificial intelligence can provide a good course description when using a well-written prompt, such as:

Learning activities, **Prompt**: You are the Subject Matter Expert for the development of XXXX course. For each unit, suggest assignments that will help students achieve the competencies, such as student presentations and case study analysis. If discussion questions and writing assignments are offered, make them as AI-proof as possible to minimize student cheating.
   a. *Note you may want to iterate this prompt with follow-up prompts directed at expanding, refining, etc.*

Final Project, **Prompt**: Suggest a final project for the course. This can be a project or a paper. It should be adjusted to be appropriate for the course level, but should demonstrate student achievement of the course competencies.
   b. *Note, this may have already been generated so this will be an iteration to refine and focus.*

This prompt, as well as others, can be found in the Addendum at the end of this book.

CHAPTER 8 - ASSESSMENT

The assessment section of the U-CAT asks that the course writer define what evidence will be used to "prove" the accomplishment of the course learning objectives. Assessment design should also reflect cognitive load considerations, since overly complex or poorly structured assessments may measure students' ability to manage extraneous load rather than their mastery of the stated learning objectives. On the U-CAT, the course learning objectives, which are typed into the appropriate cells in Section A, will automatically duplicate in the Assessment Section with an additional column for describing the method of assessment. If well written, the course objectives will be measurable, i.e., it will be possible by some method to determine whether that objective has been accomplished. In some cases, the method of assessment will be contained within the course itself. For instance, the final paper required for the course may require the student to define and apply a specific learning theory, which was one of the course objectives. In this case, besides that objective, the course writer would simply enter "satisfied by final paper." There may be more than one way to demonstrate that the objective has been met, and there may be a measurement that satisfies more than one objective. In the example above, the final paper may actually satisfy measurement of more than one of the learning objectives.

When possible, having the measurement tied directly to the course, as in the example above, is preferable; however, it is not required. In some cases, the fact that it can be measured does not necessarily mandate that it *be* directly measured. For instance, a course objective may state that upon completion of the course, the student will be able to differentiate between two philosophical perspectives. This may be evidenced in a formal paper, or it may be assumed from the amount of instruction provided. If the evidence is in the paper, that should be listed as the measure of assessment; if it is assumed from the amount of instruction, the class session(s) where that subject was discussed should be listed in the assessment category. Clear, well-structured assessments minimize extraneous load and allow students to direct their full cognitive effort toward demonstrating the germane load associated with higher-order thinking.

In some cases, the assessment may lie entirely outside the scope of the course. For instance, passing a certification exam administered by an outside agency may directly relate to a course objective. Similarly, a follow-up survey from an employer may also be considered reasonable evidence of assessment, although it may be more time-consuming and challenging to track.

Whatever the method, it is essential that each course objective has an associated assessment. When writing the course, the author should discuss the assessment portion with the individual who assigned the course to gain further insight into how the course fits into the larger academic program.

CHAPTER 9 - FAITH INTEGRATION

For institutions that place an emphasis on faith integration, the U-CAT includes a section that can be used specifically for this purpose or deleted if desired. Faith integration is a somewhat nebulous concept, with varying meanings for different institutions.

> EXCEL's faith integration model is designed to foster an authentic interaction between faith and curriculum, allowing instructors the freedom to integrate their personal faith while recognizing the primacy of the educational purpose within the context of a Christian institution. The expression of this model will be the inclusion of optional faith integration suggestions to be included in the curriculum for each week. These suggestions will appear as a separate section prior to the week's learning activities and may be used, as the instructor feels appropriate. Instructors may also choose to use their own personal method of faith integration. (Taken from the report on the Task Force from Faith Integration in Huntington University, EXCEL, 2008).

Belhaven University modified its take on Faith Integration to be an intersection of the subject with a Christian Worldview. Built into each course at Belhaven, students are challenged to differentiate how the subject would be approached from secular and Christian worldviews, with the differences discussed and held up to the light of scripture. Their curriculum development model includes the following statement: "All Belhaven University curricula prepared for Online and Adult Studies will contain three solid touch-points for providing a Christian Worldview in every course. The three touch-points will be achieved through a) instruction, and b) assessment." The touch-points are associated with specific class sessions and include lecture, discussion posts, and an essay or a portion of the final paper.

At other institutions, the definition of faith integration is more vague, with many leaving the actual interpretation of what faith integration means to the discretion of the course instructor, and with no presence in the curriculum related to the issue.

Ideally, the course writer would suggest ways, either on a weekly basis or at fixed points throughout the course, that correlate with the learning objectives, assignments, and activities to provide a meaningful intersection between faith and learning. The UCAT includes space for noting such inclusions in the curriculum. Some examples of faith integration are listed below:

- Connect the subject to a parable of Jesus.
- For nursing – in personal care use Jesus' actions.
- Evidence respect for different beliefs and cultures while contrasting with a biblical worldview.
- Follow-up on prayer requests.
- Use the Bible as a reference for specifics related to the subject.
- Pose a situation – e.g. Why did Jesus do "this."
- Pose the question, "Why is the worldview on this point different from the Christian worldview (and how is it different?)."

- Discuss challenges the student(s) may have experienced in the business world related to a Christian worldview.
- Read scripture and compare it to the subject for that week.
- In an accounting class, ask what Jesus would do in the same situation (WWJD).
- In marketing, ask questions, which compare standards to biblical principles.
- Compare/contrast Christian vs non-Christian behavior in a given situation.
- Use a resource like the Maxwell Leadership Bible for topics relative to the subject.
- Personal examples of how faith has affected our lives.
- Current events can be used effectively to demonstrate a Christian worldview and/or lack thereof.

Note that prayer at the beginning of class is notably absent from this list. The rationale for this exclusion is that the use of prayer in this manner too easily allows the instructor to "check off" the faith integration piece without genuinely addressing the intersection of the subject matter with a Christian worldview. Thus, instructors may or may not choose to begin a course with prayer but there should be purposeful thought given to the intersection of the secular and Christian worldview.

Anecdotally, most students, when interviewed, give instructors higher marks for faith integration when the class begins with prayer, even when no additional effort is made in this regard. Students also cite prayer at the beginning of class as an "expectation" of a Christian institution and that it provides a division, in most cases helpful, between their busy day and the beginning of class. While this perspective may seem like an argument for allowing prayer to fulfill the faith integration expectation, there is a greater opportunity to impact our students than simply beginning class with prayer. However, I would say that, based on personal experience, doing so is beneficial to all parties concerned. The inclusion of a space in the U-CAT allows Faith Integration to be discussed at the very least.

ARTIFICIAL INTELLIGENCE TIP

Artificial intelligence can provide a good course description when using a well-written prompt, such as:

> *Biblical Foundations Form,* **Prompt**: Assume you have a Masters of Divinity and a graduate degree in XXXXX subject. You are developing an online college course titled XXXXXXXX at the XXXXXXX level with these student competencies, create a Biblical Foundations document based on the attached, relative to the content for this course.
> a. Attach the Biblical Foundations document to the chat.
> b. Note: This is ONLY a draft and should be carefully reviewed and modified as necessary.
> c. Use this information as the foundation for developing Christian worldview touchpoints in the course.
>
> *Christian worldview,* **Prompt**: Based on the Biblical Foundations form and the topics from the course outline, create XXXX (2-4) 15 minute lectures describing how a Christian worldview differs from a secular worldview on the subject. Use supporting scripture and current examples.

This prompt, as well as others, can be found in the Addendum at the end of this book.

CHAPTER 10 – CALCULATING SEAT TIME

The standard in use to calculate seat time for higher education at the time of this publication is the Carnegie definition. This definition, accepted by most regional accrediting bodies, states that one credit hour equals one 50-minute week of in-class seat time coupled with 2 hours/week of out-of-class assignments, for a full standard semester (14-16 weeks, depending on the institution). Doing the calculation for the full semester, this equates to 750 minutes for the in-class portion (for the purpose of this example, I'm using a 15-week semester) and 1,400 minutes for the 15 weeks for the out-of-class assignments/work. This totals 2,150 minutes for one college semester credit hour. Since most courses are 3 credit hours, this totals 2,250 minutes for in-class activities and 4,200 minutes for out-of-class activities, for a total of 6,450 minutes (107.5 hours) for the semester. Seat-time calculations also intersect with cognitive load, since the number of minutes allotted for tasks must reflect not only the quantity of work but also the cognitive complexity inherent in the task.

If that is not confusing enough, consider the fact that online programs do not technically have an in-class component, which raises potential problems in defining a seat hour. These kinds of stressors are affecting the entire academy, and it is likely that significant changes are forthcoming from the accreditors to take into account these and other variations, such as Competency-Based Education (CBE).

Fortunately, in most cases, accreditors ask institutions to define a seat hour for their institution and then adhere to that definition, supported by examples. Here is where the UCAT and the UCATO can be invaluable tools for institutions that want to provide objective evidence of the appropriate rigor for their curriculum. The requirement to enter minutes related to assignments can quickly demonstrate to anyone reviewing the course whether it meets the standards set by the Institution or not.

Here is a sample credit hour definition from one university:

XXXXXX University Credit Hour Policy

Credit hours awarded for courses are determined by the faculty and academic administration in accordance with the mission and goals of XXXXXXX University. This determination is aligned with the Carnegie collegiate student credit hour, Federal definitions and requirements, and the standards, commission policies, and guidelines of XXXXXXXX, our regional accreditor. This credit hour policy guides the process for assigning credit hours for courses in the attainment of the XXXXXXX University's mission and goals.

Conforming to sound, commonly accepted best practices, the following statements are XXXXXX University's working definition and principles for credit hour determination:

- The faculty oversees the content and quality of the curriculum and is responsible for the learning outcomes; therefore, it is the responsibility of the faculty to determine course credit hour valuations.

- The number of credit hours awarded for each course is determined on the basis of time spent in classroom instruction, outside class direct instruction, and outside class student work.
- One semester hour of credit is granted for the equivalent of 750 minutes of classroom instruction and 1500 minutes of outside class student work or 2250 minutes based on a combination of classroom instruction, outside class direct instruction, and outside class student work.
- Classroom instruction and outside class direct instruction times are equivalent for the purposes of credit hour valuations.
- Classroom instruction includes the formal class meeting, supervised labs, private instruction, or any similar instructional meeting between an instructor and one or more students.
- Outside class direct instruction includes student activities that:
    - Has a planned educational purpose or outcome
    - Is facilitated by an instructor or field supervisor (guided, monitored, or observed)
    - Is graded and documented
- Outside class direct instruction activities include, but are not limited to
    - Online lectures or instruction (synchronous or asynchronous)
    - Video presentations, journal or blog writing
    - Chat rooms
    - Discussion boards
    - Field trips (which include virtual field trips)
    - Group/team-based activities
    - Online test or quizzes
    - Video conferencing
    - Virtual labs
    - Supervised field experiences

- Outside of class, student work includes course-related activities that do not qualify as direct instruction. These activities include but are not limited to reading, writing, studying, preparing, practicing and researching.
- The ratio of classroom/outside class direct instruction and outside of class student work may vary depending on the course type. The ratio of outside-of-class student work serving in support of classroom/outside-of-class direct instruction is 2:1 (two minutes of outside-of-class student work supports one minute of classroom/outside-of-class direct instruction).
- The credit hour valuation is the same for all course formats, lengths, levels, locations, and modes of delivery, which includes the traditional classroom, laboratory, online, electronic, private lessons, internships, practicums, independent study, senior thesis, or hybrid.
- The amount and level of credit hours awarded for a course will be determined according to these expectations and courses will be periodically evaluated to ensure that they meet or exceed these expectations.

Calculating the minutes required for various activities, as listed above, can also be a challenge when attempting to insert an appropriate number on the UCAT or UCATO. The list below is included, along with a recommended number of minutes for each activity. These estimated times assume a reasonable cognitive load for the type of task; tasks with higher intrinsic complexity or poorly structured instructions may exceed these estimates by adding avoidable extraneous load.

Method / Modality	Unit Measured	Normal Time to Complete ** (in minutes)

Assigned activity (unsupervised)		actual time
Practice problems - complex	per problem	30
Practice problems - simple	per problem	15
Practicum (unsupervised)		actual time
Service learning (unsupervised)		actual time
Group presentation / panel / paper (group interaction)	per week, per project	180
Plot lab data in Excel		60
Portfolio development		240
PowerPoint presentation (e.g., student-created)	per slide	20
Speech / Lecture / Debate (practice before presentation)	per minute	9
Video presentation (e.g., student-created)	per min of finished video	30
Academic, Textbook, Literary Fiction - lower-level	per page	10
Academic, Textbook, Literary Fiction - upper-level	per page	15
Popular literature reading	per page	5
Sacred literature reading	per chapter	5
Science Lab reading	per lab	30

Walk/hike (unsupervised)		actual time
Electronic research (search, narrow results, analyze source)	per source	30
Group Wiki project	per entry - 250 words	30
Interview		actual time
Library research (search, narrow results, analyze source)	per source	60
Observation		actual time
Pre-lab exam studying	per lab exam	90
Pre-quiz studying	per quiz	60
Pre-test studying	per test	180
Analysis paper	per page - 250 words	60
Annotated bibliography	per annotation	20
Case study	per page - 250 words	60
Creative writing	per page - 250 words	60
Discussion board / Forum without direct instructor participation	per discussion	90
Genogram	per generation	120
Graphic org / Concept mapping / Mind map		90

Journal / Blog writing	per entry - 250 words	30
Lab notebook and report (pre- and post-lab)	per lab	60
Lesson / sermon / speech writing	per min of finished work	15
Peer-evaluation (e.g., of posted work)	per page - 250 words	45
Reflection paper	per page - 250 words	30
Report (video, field trip, tour, interview, lab, etc.)	per page - 250 words	30
Research / Term paper - lower-level	per page - 250 words	60
Research / Term paper - upper-level	per page - 250 words	90
Résumé and cover letter		120
Self-evaluation	per page - 250 words	25
Student course evaluation	per evaluation	15
Textbook chapter outline - lower-level	per chapter	60
Textbook chapter outline - upper-level	per chapter	90
Textbook chapter questions - lower-level	per chapter	60
Textbook chapter questions - upper-level	per chapter	90

Probably the most important point is that whatever definition is used by the Institution, it must be able to be defended as applicable for each of its various delivery modalities. In other words, say what you are going to do, then do it.

ARTIFICIAL INTELLIGENCE TIP

Artificial intelligence can provide a good course description when using a well-written prompt, such as:

> *Credit Hour Calculation,* **Prompt**: Evaluate the attached syllabus and provide a breakdown of time to complete each of the items listed: lectures, readings, assignments, activities, assessments, etc., with the approximate time to complete each based on the attached credit hour definition. Show this calculation by Unit and for the total course.

This prompt, as well as others, can be found in the Addendum at the end of this book.

CHAPTER 11 - STEP-BY-STEP INSTRUCTIONS FOR USING THE CURRICULUM AUDIT

The U-CAT is a Microsoft Excel template that is divided into sections, allowing for the easy analysis of any curriculum piece using predefined standards. To use the tool, simply open the template, "save as" the name of the course being audited, and begin filling in the appropriate sections as described below.

SECTION A

In the designated spaces, include the course number, course description, and learning objectives. The course learning objectives will duplicate themselves in Section D.

SECTION B

Section B lists the in-class activities. As course writers populate Section B, they should consider the cumulative cognitive load created by the sequence of activities in each week, ensuring that complex activities are introduced with sufficient scaffolding and that extraneous load is minimized through clear and organized content.

Week	Learning Activities	SECTION B IN-Class Experience		
		Learning Outcomes	Bloom's	Style
1	I			
	II			
wk 1	III			
hmwk	IV			
hrs =	V			
0	VI			
	VII			
	VIII			

In the column marked "Learning Activities," you may replace the Roman numerals with a very brief identifier of a learning activity, or simply allow it to stand as a representative of that which is found in the faculty guide. For instance, you might replace 'I' with "Intro."

Week	Learning Activities	SECTION B IN-Class Experience		
		Learning Outcomes	Bloom's	Style
1	Intro			
	Lecture			
wk 1	Zigzag			
hmwk	Discussion			
hrs =	Video clp			
0	roundtable			
	VII			
	VIII			

In the column marked Learning Outcomes, you would connect the learning activity to one or more course learning outcomes from Section A, using the letter designation from that section. For instance, learning activity 'IV' might be associated with learning outcomes 'A' and 'C.' It is possible that each learning activity might be associated with more than one learning outcome.

Week	Learning Activities	SECTION B IN-Class Experience		
		Learning Outcomes	Bloom's	Style
1	Intro	NA		
	Lecture	A		
wk 1	Zigzag	A		
hmwk	Discussion	AD		
hrs =	Video clp	BC		
0	roundtable	A		
	VII			
	VIII			

In the column marked "Bloom's," you would connect the learning activity to one or more of the taxonomy of learning levels discussed in a previous chapter. Those are also found at the end of the UCAT for easy reference. Note that if desired, this taxonomy may easily be replaced with another.

		SECTION B IN-Class Experience		
Week	Learning Activities	Learning Outcomes	Bloom's	Style
1	Intro	NA	NA	
	Lecture	A	A	
wk 1	Zigzag	A	C	
hmwk	Discussion	AD	B	
hrs =	Video clp	BC	A	
0	roundtable	A	C	
	VII			
	VIII			

Finally, in the column marked "Style" you would connect the learning activity to a particular style of instruction as discussed in a previous chapter. Again, these are found at the end of the UCAT for easy reference and may be replaced with a different list if desired. In the case of "Style", there is usually only one letter of association, which is different from either of the columns for "Learning Outcomes" or "Bloom's", which may have more than one letter of association.

		SECTION B IN-Class Experience		
Week	Learning Activities	Learning Outcomes	Bloom's	Style
1	Intro	NA	NA	L
	Lecture	A	A	L
wk 1	Zigzag	A	C	C
hmwk	Discussion	AD	B	C
hrs =	Video clp	BC	A	M
0	roundtable	A	C	C
	VII			
	VIII			

This is what the final completed table would look like.

SECTION C

Section C is for recording the out-of-class assignments, normally referred to as homework. The U-CAT's time-tracking function becomes especially powerful when paired with cognitive load awareness, allowing course writers to monitor not only the quantity of minutes assigned but the cognitive intensity those minutes require. The lines provided are not directly connected to the same row data from Section B; however, they do connect in that they fall into weekly segments.

In the "Assignments" column, list in abbreviated form on separate rows each of the assignments for that specific week.

SECTION C		-		OUT of Class Assignments		
Assignments	Reading	Writing	Research	Total	Learning Outcome	Bloom's
Read Wilson pg 1-35				0		
Answer ? from Wilson on pg. 36				0		
				0		

In the next columns ("Reading," "Writing," "Research") insert a number in hours (e.g. 1 for one hour, 1.5 for one and a half hours, etc.) which represents the amount of time it would take for *an average student at the level matching the course number* to complete the assignment. A calculation guide is provided at

68 | Guidebook for Course Development and Assessment

the end of the UCAT. This guide is discussed in a previous chapter and may be changed at the discretion of the institution.

The "Total" column will total the three columns into one number. The sum of this column, for this particular week is shown in the box in Section B to the left of the "Learning Activities" column. The average of all the weeks is shown above Sections B and C along with a maximum and minimum hours assigned. This allows an easy gauge of the homework load across the entire course.

SECTION C		-	OUT of Class Assignments			
Assignments	Reading	Writing	Research	Total	Learning Outcome	Bloom's
Read Wilson pg 1-35	3.5			3.5		
Answer ? from Wilson on pg. 36		2		2		
Write 1 pg paper		2		2		

In the column marked Learning Outcomes, connect the homework assignment to one or more course learning outcomes from Section A, using the letter designation from that section. It is possible that an assignment will be associated with more than one learning outcome.

SECTION C - OUT of Class Assignments					
Assignments	Reading	Writing	Research	Total	Learning Outcome	Bloom's
Read Wilson pg 1-35	3.5			3.5	A	
Answer ? from Wilson on pg. 36		2		2	A,C	
Write 1 pg paper		2		2	B	

In the column marked "Bloom's," you would connect the homework assignment to one or more of the taxonomy of learning levels discussed in a previous chapter. Again, these are also found at the end of the curriculum audit for easy reference.

SECTION C - OUT of Class Assignments					
Assignments	Reading	Writing	Research	Total	Learning Outcome	Bloom's
Read Wilson pg 1-35	3.5			3.5	A	A
Answer ? from Wilson on pg. 36		2		2	A,C	B,C
Write 1 pg paper		2		2	B	C

This is what the completed section would look like.

SECTION D

This section provides the course writer the opportunity to demonstrate how each of the course objectives will be assessed. When reviewing assessments in Section D, course writers should ensure that the cognitive load required to complete each assessment aligns with both the level of the course and the intended learning outcomes. This topic is discussed in more detail in a previous chapter.

SECTION E

This section provides the course writer with the opportunity to suggest faith integration activities that align with the week's learning objectives. This topic is discussed in more detail in a previous chapter.

CHAPTER 12 - ONLINE VARIATIONS

Online instructional design presents some unique variations, and therefore, I have created an alternative version of the U-CAT, labeled the U-CATO, to address these differences. The U-CATO can be downloaded at https://tinyurl.com/236dcz8r . The focus of this section will be to discuss some of the components of online instruction that differ from those in the classroom, as well as how to design and evaluate a course using the U-CATO to ensure quality. The course writer preparing material for an online course would be well advised to complement this material with other curriculum design materials specifically designed for online instructors.

A significant variation exists between the online and classroom models in terms of learning activities. A purely online environment removes from the instructor's toolbox one of the most powerful tools – the ability to gauge student body language and garner non-verbal feedback to modify the flow of the instructional process. Because of this, both the curriculum and the instructor have to make extra effort at establishing a "presence" within the online course. Some activities, which help establish this presence, include:

- Introduction to the course in audio or video format.

- Weekly summary is reinforced either on the discussion board, through an audio recording of the instructor, or a video clip.
- Audio feedback on assignments, which can be inserted directly into MS Word files or the LMS
- Active involvement in a non-class-related discussion forum and a willingness to share, appropriately, personal information.
- Make sure the Instructor's profile is updated in the LMS, including a recent picture.

Additionally, the online environment requires instructors to prepare their materials significantly in advance of the actual class offering so that they can be uploaded to the course site. This means much less flexibility/spontaneity than is found in the on-site classroom experience. For at least these two reasons, many on-site instructors have found teaching online to be an unpleasant experience. Some have estimated that building an online course takes approximately 180 hours from start to finish, all of which must be completed before the class even begins.

Yet, there are tremendous benefits for those who can accept these boundaries. One of the benefits is the greater demand on students to become actively involved in the learning process through the discussion boards. Part of the expanded interaction comes because of stated requirements for posting; however, there can be seen in most online courses an amazing "blooming" of some students who would normally sit quietly through an on-site course. This kind of experience can be equally exciting for the online instructor as it is for the on-site instructor, who enjoys the classroom buzz. When thoughtfully designed, online structures can also support germane load by organizing content clearly, sequencing learning steps, and reducing extraneous barriers inherent in digital navigation.

So, what does an online course look like, and how should you think about constructing an online course? Regardless of your learning platform, there are several components that can be used to construct a dynamic online experience for students, which equals, if not surpasses, the on-site experience. Before we look at these components, we need to go over some basic vocabulary:

- Learning Management System (LMS) - The LMS is commonly an institutional decision based on a variety of factors such as cost, bandwidth, support, etc. Most LMS systems work pretty much the same, so if you learn one system, it probably would not take long to grasp the functioning of a different system. These LMS systems allow students to log in to a closed system and access a specific course site, which contains all the necessary components related to that course. Most of these elements will come from the course writer, but there may be some standard pieces that have been established by the institution to be present in all course sites. An example would be a generic discussion forum for students to "discuss" topics unrelated to the course.
- Synchronous – courses, which are synchronous, are courses in which everyone is present at the same time. Most online courses do not fit this description since one of the benefits of online instruction is the ability to work it around different work/life commitments. However, online courses may have a synchronous component, which may take the form

of a video conference at scheduled points throughout the course. These synchronous events may or may not be required, are typically recorded, and available for students to review as needed. In the early days of online communication, synchronous interactions were a standard part of the model, typically using either chat or video conferencing. That model was gradually discontinued in favor of the asynchronous model, largely due to complications in geography and internet infrastructure, which could not handle the necessary bandwidth for a quality synchronous experience. Although bandwidth issues are largely in the past, asynchronous remains the most common model for online courses. However, there has recently been a growing awareness that incorporating a synchronous component into the online class may contribute to student engagement and possibly retention.

- Asynchronous – courses, which are asynchronous, are courses in which students and instructors interact regularly throughout a fixed period, but not necessarily at the same time. In an asynchronous course, the instruction may be broken into weeklong segments, but there are few restrictions on when to participate in the course experience. In the asynchronous environment, students and instructors will rarely be "online" at the same time, but can still contribute to a meaningful interaction. The asynchronous format is perfect for geographically dispersed participants who can log in to the course site at the times and places that fit their schedule.
- Static – online courses that are static have little or no requirements for instructor/student interaction and perform very much like stand-alone

independent study, or what used to be called correspondence courses. These courses are best used for training purposes and can be quite effective in providing training for specific skills or tasks.

- Hybrid: Refers to courses within a program that consist of entire courses delivered either fully online or fully on-ground; however, both types of courses may make up the program. For example, course XX1 is only offered online, while XX2 is only offered on-ground[2].

- Blended: Courses contain both online and on-ground components, which reduces the number of on-ground sessions. For example, the course may meet on weeks 1, 3, 5, & 7 on ground and weeks 2, 4, 6, and 8 online.

- Augmented: On-ground courses, which include aspects of online course delivery, e.g., discussion boards, but do not necessarily affect the number of on-ground sessions, nor the length of the on-ground session.

- Virtual Synchronous (VS): Refers to courses that are delivered entirely through video conference. VS courses have aspects of both the on-ground and online delivery modalities. In a typical design, these courses would meet at regular intervals, e.g. weekly, on the same date and at the same time. The VS course would be augmented by the use of an LMS to carry the bulk of the instructional content. The advantage of the VS course is the regular presence of a live instructor and the interaction

---

[2] Hybrid and Blended terms are often switched by different institutions or combined in some way or confused with the Augmented format. There is little clarity within the Academy as a whole on how they terms are used

with other students in the "virtual" classroom, while offering some of the flexibility of the online course.

The following components are used in creating an online class. Every component of an online course—from navigation to instructions to media design—should be evaluated for its impact on intrinsic, extraneous, and germane load.

- Discussion forum – the discussion forum is also known as a threaded discussion because it ties or "threads" online posts[3] together so that it is recognizable as a conversation. This "tying" or "thread" is found in the common subject line and posting structure which cascades under an initial comment or question.
    - Discussion forums are the most prominent feature of online courses. In a discussion forum, the instructor posts a question to the course site and students respond to that question and to each other's posts, creating a virtual discussion. Since this usually happens asynchronously, students may post at any time, day or night, throughout the week, and have the luxury of taking time to think through their response and even research supporting documentation, which can also be a stated requirement of the initial question. For instructors, the discussion forums are the primary source of opportunity to gauge learning by reading

---

[3] "Posts" in the context of an online discussion form mean the typed entries students make in response either to the question or in reply to another student's post. Posts can be done in real-time while connected to the internet or composed offline using a word processor and then pasted into the discussion board.

students' posts. They can also be the bane of an instructor's existence, as every student will post to every question and often engage in full discussions, requiring significant faculty time to read and evaluate.
- Variations to the discussion forum can include the possibility of blocking other students from viewing other students posts until they have made their initial post. The advantage of this variation is that it requires each student to fully answer the question without being tempted to paraphrase another student's post or simply say "ditto."
- Discussion forums work well in either low or high-bandwidth scenarios.
- There are two keys to effectively using the discussion forum to facilitate student learning.
  - The first is to construct good questions. The components of a good question include:
    - Being stated in such a way that it requires several lines to adequately answer the question.
    - Being provocative toward encouraging students to think critically.
    - Opens the door for further inquiry
  - The second is to have clearly stated expectations for student responses. Some examples of expectations are:
    - Require the answer to be a certain number of lines or words in length.

- Require the answer to include a link to a supporting web document, which applies to the subject.
- Require that students make their initial post early enough in the week that other students can reply.
- Require students to reply meaningfully to other students for full credit.

- Lectures – Lectures for online courses are not the same as classroom lectures and take many forms. In all of these cases, the major distinction of the online course is that this material is prepared before the course even begins and is posted to the course site. Making last-minute corrections can be done, but it can be technically complicated and often causes confusion. Some of the variations are:
    - Audio files (mp3), which the instructor records and the student can download and listen to in a variety of ways.
    - Video files that the instructor or SME records and uploads to the course site. Video files can also be used as an introduction to a topic with additional connected assignments or as an example of the principle under discussion.
    - White papers that the instructor writes for the student to read.

  Depending on the amount of media, lectures can work well in either low or high-bandwidth.

- Media Clips – these can be assigned from a variety of sources and used to introduce discussions, form the basis of a quiz, etc.

- Quizzes/Tests – these are easily constructed for the online course site and can have great benefit if used wisely. An example would be to introduce each week with a pre-quiz, which is not counted toward the grade. If the pre-quiz is passed successfully at the level set by the instructor, then the program can unlock the key for taking the end-of-week quiz. Online quizzes can be in almost any format. If clearly pre-defined answers are identified (e.g. multiple choice, true/false, short answer, matrix, ranking, etc.), the course site will automatically grade the quiz and post it to the course gradebook. Unless there is a media component to the quiz/test, these generally work in either low or high-bandwidth scenarios. In many cases, an institution will employ third-party vendors to ensure quizzes/tests are completed with integrity.
- Glossary – just like it sounds, but with an online benefit, glossaries are areas of the course site to which students can be assigned to contribute. The resource then becomes available to the whole class.
- Wikis – a wiki is a group workspace, which can be used for a variety of purposes such as developing a group paper, building a group knowledge base (e.g. Wikipedia), etc. The use of wikis is beginning to be recognized as one of the strongest resources for online learning components since it is a highly collaborative space. Problems associated with wikis usually revolve around what makes it the greatest benefit – i.e., its collaborative nature.
- Collaborative workspaces – Similar to Wikis are the collaborative workspaces now found in products like Google Drive and Microsoft Office 365. These tools and others like them enable students to work on

the same document, spreadsheet, or presentation simultaneously from geographically diverse locations. This makes team projects and collaboration possible in an online environment.

- Questionnaires and Surveys – since the course site can summarize this data on the fly, these can be useful tools for getting an understanding of student experience/opinion on various course-related topics.
- Assigned homework – usually in the form of reading a textbook and providing written answers to specific questions. This can also include research using the Institution's digital resources and writing papers. In most cases, this type of assignment is completed by the student offline and submitted to a class "dropbox" (digital storage center) and can be a single file or multiple files.
- Textbook websites are becoming more and more popular and some online courses take advantage of these resources to augment some aspect of the course.
- Open Educational Resources (OER) – OER is expanding in availability. These resources are typically free, or nearly so, to students and faculty and available in digital format, primarily, which makes them ideal for online. OER is growing in popularity, but has not fully reached its potential, mostly due to the diversity of subjects, lack of peer review for quality, and fewer, if any, instructor resources.
- Augmented Instructor Resources – These resources are now readily available for almost any textbook and provide the instructor with a wealth of additional materials to supplement their teaching. These

include, but are not limited to, slide sets, suggested video clips, worksheets, lecture notes, and more.

USING THE U-CATO TO HELP DEVELOP AND AUDIT THE ONLINE COURSE

The use of the U-CATO for online curriculum is the same as for the in-class curriculum, as described in the previous chapter for Sections A, D, and E; I will not repeat this information here[4]. The major departure is in Sections B and C. Since there is no discernible separation from the "In-class experience" and "Out of class assignments", these two sections have been combined for the U-CATO and labeled Section BC. Another variation is the time expectations listed on the U-CATO for the various levels. This change has been made because the amount of assigned homework measured for the U-CAT did not include time spent in class (seat time), which has to be part of the overall calculation for the U-CATO. The table below outlines the proposed differences between the two tools. Keep in mind that these time allocations may easily be adjusted by the institution according to its own guidelines.

	On-site course - weekly expectations for completion of Homework (does not include seat time in class)	Online course - weekly expectations for completion of all work

---

[4] In developing the online course, the same process described under "Weekly Objectives" found on page 17-20 can be followed with great effect. Although the assignments and activities may vary due to the nature of the online environment, the actual process remains basically the same, i.e. what assignments will facilitate learning which accomplishes the weekly objectives and which activities will best reinforce that learning.

Freshmen 100 level courses	7-9 hours	8.5 – 10.5 hours
Sophomore 200 level courses	8-10 hours	9.5 – 11.5 hours
Junior 300 level courses	9-11 hours	10.5 – 12.5 hours
Senior 400 level courses	10-12 hours	11.5 – 13.5 hours
Graduate >400 level courses	11-13 hours	12.5 – 14.5 hours

Keeping in mind the various components for online courses described briefly above, the next step is to determine which of those will best facilitate student learning within the context of the weekly learning objectives. The U-CATO's role is to allow the writer/instructor to evaluate how well their course accomplishes:

1. The goals for balance (i.e. time spent per week).
2. How does each week address the overall course objectives?
3. The rigor of the assignments/activities using a learning taxonomy.

An example of the U-CATO used for Week #1 for Biblical Covenants is shown below. Note that calculating the time for reading and responding to discussion forum questions may be difficult to calculate.

Week		SECTION BC - list times in hourly increments or portions thereof (e.g. 90 minutes = 1.5 hours)						
		Assignments/Activities	Listening/Reading	Writing	Other	Total	Learning Outcome	Bloom's
1	I	Introduction			.75	.75	NA	NA
	II	Read Ch. 1 / Answer ???	1.2	1.5		2.7	A	B

		Read Article & Answer ??	.5	1		1.5	B	B
wk 1	III							
	IV	Read Lecture L1L1	1			1	A	A
hrs =	V	Read Lecture L1L2	1			1	A	B
10.45	VI	Discussion #1		1.5		1	NA	NA
	VII	Discussion #2		1.5		1.5	A	B
	VIII	Discussion #3		1.5		1.5	A	B

For more information, refer to Chapter 9 – Calculating Seat Time.

You can see that the expected time commitment for this example for the week's instructional experiences is projected to be 10.45 hours. The various columns show how the time is distributed. The Learning Outcome column identifies each activity as it relates to the learning outcomes for the course – again, this forces the developer to ensure that all activities are aligned toward the goal of that course. The Bloom's column also helps the developer consider their assignments and expectations in light of critical thinking standards.

CHAPTER 13 - CONCLUSION

Curriculum development is, at its heart, an act of stewardship. It requires us to take seriously the responsibility entrusted to us: shaping learning environments that allow students to grow intellectually, professionally, and personally. The tools, models, and principles described throughout this book point toward a singular aim—the intentional design of courses that promote deep, meaningful learning within a coherent educational philosophy.

This work is not accidental. Effective curriculum is never the result of simply compiling content, nor is it achieved by relying on past habits or the patterns we observed from our own teachers. Rather, it emerges when the course writer steps back to consider the whole landscape of learning and then crafts each element to serve the student's growth. Course descriptions define boundaries. Learning objectives lay the foundation. Taxonomies guide the cognitive trajectory. Assignments and learning activities sculpt the learning experience. Assessment measures alignment and integrity. Faith integration illuminates meaning, purpose, and worldview. Calculating seat time ensures appropriate rigor. The U-CAT brings these elements together into a unified, reviewable system.

The introduction of cognitive load theory into this edition adds another essential dimension. It reminds us that the student's ability to learn is shaped not only by what we teach, but by *how* we structure the mental effort required for learning. When we manage intrinsic load carefully, reduce extraneous load wherever possible, and cultivate germane load purposefully, we create conditions where students can engage deeply rather than merely survive. Attention to cognitive load is an expression of care for the learner—and an affirmation that rigor and compassion are not opposites but partners in responsible teaching.

At the same time, emerging technologies—particularly generative AI—offer new opportunities for creativity, efficiency, and instructional clarity. But these tools also require discernment. AI can support curriculum development, but it cannot replace the wisdom, vision, and pedagogical judgment of a thoughtful educator. Used rightly, it becomes a companion in the design process, not a substitute for it. The goal is not to automate the educator's work, but to amplify it—so that more of our energy can be directed toward the irreplaceable human dimensions of teaching and learning.

As you continue to develop courses, evaluate syllabi, or lead curriculum teams, I invite you to approach this work as both craft and calling. Each decision—whether about sequencing, objectives, assignments, or assessments—shapes the educational journey of real students. They will carry your course with them into workplaces, ministry, relationships, and the unfolding of their own purpose. When we design with intentionality, clarity, and student-centered vision, we participate in a larger formation story—one that extends well beyond the boundaries of any classroom.

In that spirit, may the models and tools offered in these pages serve you not merely as technical instruments, but as aids to thoughtful, transformative teaching. May your courses become places where minds are shaped, character is strengthened, and learners discover the joy of understanding. And may your work as an educator reflect the deep truth that teaching is, ultimately, an act of service — an opportunity to invest in the flourishing of others.

The task before us is ongoing. Curriculum is not static; it grows as our students grow, as disciplines evolve, and as new insights emerge. But with a clear philosophy, a coherent process, and the courage to evaluate our work honestly, we can continue to build courses — and programs — that honor both the learner and the learning.

You now have the tools. The next step belongs to you.

CONCEPTUAL MODEL FOR CURRICULUM DEVELOPMENT INCLUDING AND USING GENERATIVE AI FOR CURRICULUM DEVELOPMENT

Faculty and Instructional Designers are tasked with creating transformative learning experiences that prepare students for the complexities of modern society. This document outlines a four-part conceptual framework for curriculum development, integrating Subject Matter Competency, a Christian Worldview, Critical Thinking Skills, and Generative AI, along with suggestions on how to utilize generative AI to support curriculum development. These elements are designed to work synergistically, fostering intellectual growth, ethical reasoning, and practical skills that align with the demands of the 21st century.

By embedding these components into course competencies and learning activities, this model ensures that students develop a strong foundation in their field of study. It also equips them to navigate societal challenges with integrity, critical insight, and technological fluency.

THE FOUR-PART MODEL

1. Subject Matter Competency

>Definition and Importance: Subject matter competency ensures that students develop a deep understanding of the core knowledge and skills within their discipline. This foundational element is critical for professional success and lifelong learning.

Implementation: Course competencies should clearly articulate the specific knowledge and skills students must master. Learning activities should include scaffolded assignments, case studies, and assessments that progressively build expertise.

Connection to Society: Mastery of subject matter empowers students to make meaningful contributions to their professions and communities, addressing real-world problems with confidence and precision.

2. Christian Worldview

Definition and Importance: A Christian worldview (CWV) offers a moral and ethical framework through which students can critically evaluate their discipline. It emphasizes values such as stewardship, compassion, and justice, encouraging students to consider how their work serves the greater good.

Implementation: Course competencies should include reflective objectives that challenge students to explore how their discipline intersects with Christian principles. Learning activities might involve ethical dilemmas, discussions on faith and vocation, or service-learning projects.

Connection to Society: By integrating a CWV, students are prepared to approach their careers with a sense of purpose and responsibility, making decisions that reflect integrity and a commitment to societal well-being.

3. Critical Thinking Skills

Definition and Importance: Critical thinking involves analyzing, evaluating, and synthesizing information to make reasoned decisions. It is a cornerstone of intellectual development and problem-solving.

Implementation: Course competencies should emphasize analytical reasoning, argumentation, and evidence-based decision-making. Learning activities might include debates, research projects, and problem-based learning scenarios.

Connection to Society: In a world of rapid change and information overload, critical thinking empowers students to discern truth, challenge assumptions, and devise innovative solutions to complex challenges.

4. Generative AI

Definition and Importance: Generative AI (Gen AI) refers to artificial intelligence systems capable of creating content, such as text, images, and code. Familiarity with Gen AI is essential for students to remain competitive in a technology-driven world.

Implementation: Course competencies should include objectives related to both the use and critical evaluation of Gen AI tools. Learning activities might involve using AI for research, exploring its ethical implications, and assessing its impact on the discipline.

Connection to Society: By engaging with Gen AI, students gain practical experience with cutting-edge technology while developing an understanding of its societal implications, such as bias, privacy, and the future of work.

HOW THE MODEL FACILITATES STUDENT PREPAREDNESS

This four-part model equips students with the knowledge, skills, and ethical grounding needed to thrive in a rapidly evolving society. Here's how:

Holistic Development: By combining technical expertise (subject matter competency) with ethical reasoning (informed by a Christian worldview), students are prepared to make meaningful contributions to their fields while upholding moral principles.

Adaptability: Critical thinking skills enable students to navigate uncertainty, solve problems creatively, and adapt to new challenges.

Technological Fluency: Experience with Generative AI ensures that students are not only consumers of technology but also informed critics and innovators who understand its potential and limitations.

Ethical Leadership: The integration of a Christian worldview fosters leaders who prioritize justice, compassion, and stewardship in their professional and personal lives.

Summary

This four-part model for curriculum development—integrating subject matter competency, a Christian worldview, critical thinking skills, and Generative AI—ensures that students are well-prepared for the demands of contemporary society. This approach prepares students for professional success and empowers them to lead lives of purpose and impact.

ADDENDUM: USING GENERATIVE AI IN CURRICULUM DEVELOPMENT

PROMPTS FOR COURSE DEVELOPMENT:

The prompts listed below are meant to be used in the sequence provided. This provides the AI with a solid foundation of information to build upon for future iterations and developments. However, using any of the prompts will provide helpful information if you remember to follow the CRAFT framework for constructing effective prompts.

The CRAFT framework is a method for creating effective prompts for AI language models. It stands for:

- C - Context: Provide relevant background information – the more the better.
- R - Role: Specify the role the AI should assume, in this case identify as a Subject Matter Expert
- A - Action: Clearly state what task or action you want the AI to perform.
- F - Format: Define the desired format for the AI's response.
- T - Tone: Indicate the appropriate tone or style for the response – in this case academic

After receiving each response, you may need to make minor/major alterations to the subsequent prompts to allow for new information or desired iterations.

NOTE: Generative AI can be prone to providing incorrect and/or off-topic answers to prompts. The developer must use critical thinking skills to discern when this happens and take corrective measures.

PROMPTS

2. *If the course doesn't have a description,* **Prompt**: Act as if you have a Ph.D in XXX and are developing an online college course titled XXX, at the XXX (Freshman, Sophomore, Junior, Senior, Graduate, Doctoral) level, create a 3-6 sentence description. The description should be professional but interesting enough to encourage student enrollment.

2. *Textbook selection,* **Prompt**: Act as if you have a Ph.D in XXX and are developing an online college course titled XXX, at the XXX (Freshman, Sophomore, Junior, Senior, Graduate, Doctoral) level, suggest three textbooks to choose from for this course. The choices should all be the most recent publications, having been published within the last three years.
   a. Once you select a textbook, make sure it is the most recent version. WE CAN ONLY USE THE MOST RECENT VERSIONS FOR COURSE DEVELOPMENT

3. *Course Competencies,* **Prompt**: Act as if you have a Ph.D in XXX and are developing an online college course titled XXX, at the XXX (Freshman, Sophomore, Junior, Senior, Graduate, Doctoral) level, suggest 8-10 Student competencies that complete this sentence: At the conclusion of this course, the student should be able to. Do not use the word understand. One of the course competencies should focus on integrating the course into a Christian worldview. One of the competencies should be the ability to effectively utilize generative AI in the subject area.
   a. Note that you must carefully edit these competencies to match your vision for the course.

4. *Biblical Foundations Form,* **Prompt**: Assume you have a Masters of Divinity and a graduate degree in XXXXX subject. You are developing an online college course titled XXXXXXX at the XXXXXXX level with these student competencies, create a Biblical Foundations document based on the attached, relative to the content for this course.
   a. Attach the Biblical Foundations document to the chat.
   b. Note: This is ONLY a draft and should be carefully reviewed and modified as necessary.

c. Use this information as the foundation for developing Christian worldview touchpoints in the course.

5. *Course Outline,* **Prompt***:* Act as if you have a Ph.D in XXX and are developing an online college course titled XXX, at the XXX (Freshman, Sophomore, Junior, Senior, Graduate, Doctoral) level, with these student competencies (if you have modified the competencies or are not in a continous chat, you will need to list them), lay out a course outline for XXXXX weeks. Include 3-5 Unit objectives for each week. The textbook will be XXXXXXX. Include assigned readings in the course outline. Include additional readings from scholarly journals and contemporary case studies where applicable.
    a. *Note you may want to iterate this prompt with follow-up prompts directed at expanding, refining, etc.*

3. *Learning activities,* **Prompt***:* You are the Subject Matter Expert for the development of XXXX course. For each unit, suggest assignments that will help students achieve the competencies, such as student presentations and case study analysis. If discussion questions and writing assignments are offered, make them as AI-proof as possible to minimize student cheating.
    a. *Note you may want to iterate this prompt with follow-up prompts directed at expanding, refining, etc.*

4. *Final Project,* **Prompt***:* Suggest a final project for the course. This can be a project or a paper. It should be adjusted to be appropriate for the course level, but should demonstrate student achievement of the course competencies.
    a. *Note, this may have already been generated so this will be an iteration to refine and focus.*

5. *Syllabus,* **Prompt***:* Use the course description, course competencies, course outline, learning activities, and final project to construct a whole course syllabus based on the attached template.
    a. *Note, you can either paste in the material from previous prompts or save them to individual documents and attach them.*

b. Note, you will need to attach a syllabus template for the prompt to follow. The template should have a designated space in each unit for the lecture.

6. *Lectures **Prompt***: Create PowerPoint presentations for each week that expand on the outlined topics. These should be 20-30 slides with the smallest font size set at 26 points. Use as many graphics as possible and minimize text. Provide speaking notes to accompany the PowerPoint.

7. *Christian worldview,* ***Prompt***: Based on the Biblical Foundations form and the topics from the course outline, create XXXX (2-4) 15 minute lectures describing how a Christian worldview differs from a secular worldview on the subject. Use supporting scripture and current examples.

8. *Credit Hour Calculation,* ***Prompt***: Evaluate the attached syllabus and provide a breakdown of time to complete each of the items listed: lectures, readings, assignments, activities, assessments, etc., with the approximate time to complete each based on the attached credit hour definition. Show this calculation by Unit and for the total course.

BIBLIOGRAPHY

Anderson, Lorin W., David R.Krathwohl, Peter Airasian, Kathleen Cruikshank, Richard Mayer, Paul Pintrich, James Raths, Merlin Wittrock. A Taxonomy for Learning, Teaching, and Assessing: A Revision of Bloom's Taxonomy of Educational Objectives. New York: Longman, 2001.

Barkley, Elizabeth F., K. Patricia Cross, Claire Howell Major. Collaborative Learning Techniques: A Handbook for College Faculty. San Francisco: Josey Bass, 2005.

Collison, George, Bonnie Elbaum, Sarah Haavink, Robert Tinker. Facilitating Online Learning: Effective Strategies for Moderators. Madison, WI: 2000, 2000.

Elbaum, Bonnie, Cynthia McIntyre, and Alese Smith. Essential Elements: Prepare, Design, and Teach Your Online Course. Madison, WI: Atwood Publishing, 2002.

Gibson, Chere Campbell. Distance Learners in Higher Education: Institutional Responses for Quality Outcomes. Madison, WI: Atwood Publishing, 1998.

Pallof, Rena M., Keith Pratt. Building Learning Communities in Cyberspace. San Francisco: Josey Bass, 1999.

Richardson, Will. Blogs, Wikis, Podcasts, and Other Powerful Web Tools for Classrooms. Thousand Oaks, CA: Corwin Press, 2009.

Richlin, Laurie. Blueprint for Learning: Constructing College Courses to Facilitate, Assess, and Document Learning. Sterling: Stylus, 2006.

Vella, Jane. <u>Taking Learning to Task: Creative Strategies for Teaching Adults.</u> San Francisco: Jossey-Bass, 2001.

Wilkinson, Bruce. <u>The 7 Laws of the Learner: How to Teach Almost Anything to Practically Anyone</u>. Sisters, Oregon: Multnomah Press, 1992.

www.ingramcontent.com/pod-product-compliance
Lightning Source LLC
Chambersburg PA
CBHW080604170426
43196CB00017B/2903